SOLDIERS' DOGS

by Meish Goldish

Consultant: Ron Aiello
President of the United States War Dogs Association
Marine Scout Dog Handler

New York, New York

Credits

Cover and Title Page, © Pascal Guyot/AFP/Getty Images; Cover TR, © Bryce Harper/Getty Images; Cover CR, © Marine Corporal Megan Leavey; Cover BR, © Associated Press; TOC, © Pascal Guyot/ AFP/Getty Images; 4, © John Moore/Getty Images; 5, © Everett Collection Inc / Alamy; 6, © LCpl Jorge A. Ortiz; 7, © CPL Mark Webster/Crown Copyright 2011; 8, © Bryce Harper/Getty Images; 9T, © U.S. Navy/Photographer's Mate Airman Ian W. Anderson; 9B, © Robbin Cresswell/USAF; 10, © Crown Copyright 2012; 11, © Dave Husbands/Crown; 12, © Jon Rabiroff/Stars and Stripes; 13, © Maurice McDonald/Pool/Reuters/Corbis; 14, © Master Sgt. Darrell Lewis/US Air Force; 15, © PASCAL GUYOT/AFP/Getty Images; 16, © B. Dawn Yoder; 17, © Baz Ratner/Reuters; 18, © Associated Press; 19, © Associated Press; 20, © SWNS.COM; 21, © SWNS.com; 22, © Marine Corporal Megan Leavey; 23, © Seth Wenig/Associated Press; 24, © ALI JASIM/Reuters/Corbis; 25, © Isaac L Koval/iStockphoto; 26, © Patsy Swendson; 27, © Patsy Swendson; 28, © Def VID / Demotix/ Demotix/Demotix/Corbis; 29TR, © Eric Isselée/Shutterstock; 29TL, © Irina oxilixo Danilova/ Shutterstock; 29BR, © Eric Isselée/Shutterstock; 29BL, © cynoclub/Shutterstock.

Publisher: Kenn Goin
Editorial Director: Adam Siegel
Creative Director: Spencer Brinker
Design: Dawn Beard Creative
Photo Researcher: We Research Pictures, LLC

Library of Congress Cataloging-in-Publication Data

Goldish, Meish.
  Soldiers' dogs / by Meish Goldish ; consultant, Ron Aiello.
    p. cm. — (Dog heroes)
  Includes bibliographical references and index.
  Audience: Ages 7-12.
  ISBN 978-1-61772-696-5 (library binding) — ISBN 1-61772-696-6 (library binding)
  1. Dogs—War use—United States—Juvenile literature. 2. Dogs—War use—Afghanistan— Juvenile literature. 3. Dogs—War use—Iraq—Juvenile literature. I. Aiello, Ron. II. Title.
  UH100.G64 2012
  355.4'24—dc23
                              2012032064

For more information, write to Bearport Publishing Company, Inc., 45 West 21st Street, Suite 3B, New York, New York 10010. Printed in the United States of America.

10 9 8 7 6 5 4 3 2 1

Table of Contents

Sniffing Out Danger

In 2011, British soldiers were searching a **compound** in Afghanistan for **explosives**. Private Andrew Duff, a dog **handler**, was on **patrol** with an English springer spaniel named Jack. The dog was trained to sniff out bombs that the enemy might have hidden in the area.

This bomb-sniffing dog, Toby, is an English springer spaniel. He is searching for explosives with British troops in Afghanistan.

As Private Duff was about to take his next step, Jack suddenly stopped and sat down in front of him. It was the dog's way of letting his handler know that bombs were buried just ahead. Thanks to Jack's sharp sense of smell, the bombs were found before they could do any harm. Private Duff later said of Jack, "To this day I am certain that he saved my life and those around me."

A U.S. soldier and his dog search for weapons in the mountains of Afghanistan.

A country's **military** often uses dogs as bomb sniffers because of their amazing ability to pick up **scents**. A dog's nose has up to 220 million **cells** for smelling, compared to only 5 million in a human's nose.

A Famous Hero

Jack's discovery of the hidden bombs wasn't the first time the brave **canine** had saved Private Duff's life. On at least nine occasions while the pair worked together in Afghanistan, the dog found hidden bombs and warned his handler in time. Private Duff said that the springer spaniel had saved his life "more times than I care to think about."

This bomb was uncovered by soldiers in Afghanistan.

The explosives Jack found are called improvised explosive devices, or IEDs. They are homemade bombs that an enemy makes to attack soldiers.

Jack's bomb-sniffing skills became so well known that he appeared with Private Duff on the cover of the British magazine *Country Life* in December 2011. Private Duff said, "Jack's appetite for searching is **immeasurable**. Whenever he's out of his kennel, he's working, whether I've asked him to or not. He loves it."

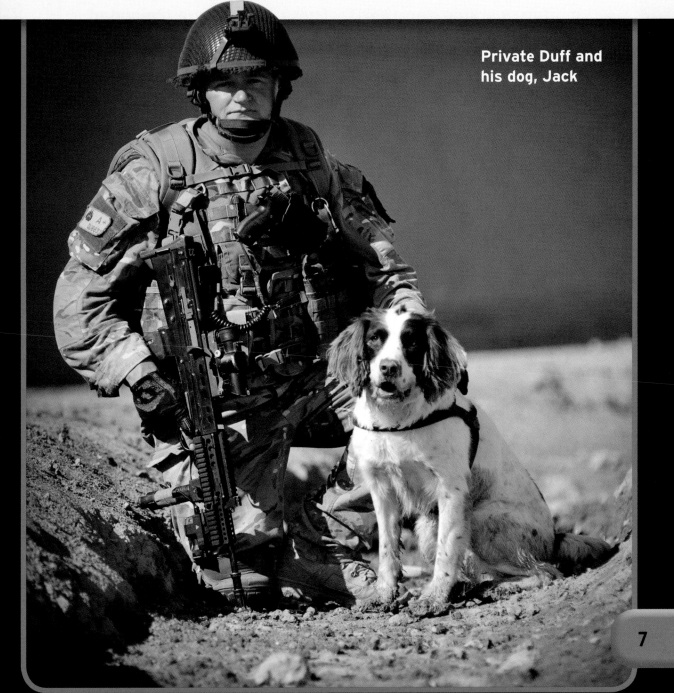

Private Duff and his dog, Jack

Trained for Success

Bomb-sniffing dogs like Jack are part of many militaries around the world. In the United States, a dog that serves in the **armed forces** is officially known as a military working dog (MWD). These canines are trained at Lackland Air Force Base in San Antonio, Texas, for about eleven weeks before they start to work.

Ben is being trained at Lackland Air Force Base to sniff out explosives hidden in a suitcase.

During the eleven-week training period, an MWD lives with a handler who trains, feeds, and grooms the animal. By spending lots of time together, the two are able to bond.

During training, each dog works closely with its handler. The dog learns how to sniff out bombs that are hidden from sight. The canine is taught to recognize the enemy and to bite on command. The dog is also trained to attack anyone who is harming its handler.

While at Lackland, handlers fire weapons near their dogs so that the animals get used to the sound of gunfire.

Handlers at Lackland Air Force Base also teach their dogs to obey basic commands such as "sit" and "come."

A Loyal Partner

A military dog is taught to remain **loyal** to its handler at all times. A yellow Labrador retriever named Tam proved how this loyalty can save a soldier's life. In 2011, Tam was on patrol in Afghanistan with his handler, Lance Corporal James Wilkinson of the British Army. Suddenly, an IED exploded. Black smoke quickly filled the air, making it difficult to see.

Before working with Tam, Wilkinson patrolled parts of Afghanistan with Jamie, another bomb-sniffing dog.

Wilkinson was badly wounded by **shrapnel** that sprayed into his hip, leg, and stomach. Luckily, Tam remained by his side, barking loudly. As a result, soldiers were able to find Wilkinson quickly in the dark smoke. They put a **tourniquet** on his leg to stop the bleeding and then rushed him to a hospital. Doctors said that if Wilkinson had arrived one minute later, he would have died. Tam had helped save his handler's life.

Lance Corporal James Wilkinson on patrol in Afghanistan

Tam's barking not only drew soldiers to the scene, but also brought Wilkinson back to **consciousness** after he passed out during the blast. Wilkinson said, "Tam kept on barking to keep me awake. He helped save my life."

Stray Helpers

Most dogs that aid soldiers are trained MWDs. However, some **stray dogs** also help the military. In Iraq and Afghanistan, for example, many homeless dogs roam the streets. Often, soldiers bring them back to their **base** and care for them. Some strays even join the soldiers on patrol, where they might find or scare away the enemy.

Although it is against U.S. military rules for a soldier to **adopt** a stray animal, many army officials allow the practice. They know that a pet can lift the spirits of the soldiers and comfort them as they struggle to cope with the hardships of war.

U.S. Army Specialist Jimmy Labbee feeds Smoke, a stray dog kept on a base in Afghanistan.

Captain Matt Taylor, a member of the U.S. **Marine Corps**, knows the value of a stray dog. In Afghanistan, his **unit** adopted a puppy that they named Alice. Taylor said that when a soldier comes back to the base, the dog is there to "give you a lick, put her head on your lap, and remind you there is something nice in the world, too."

A soldier plays with a stray dog during his patrol in Baghdad, Iraq.

Lost and Found

Whether dogs are strays or trained MWDs, they often risk their lives for the soldiers they accompany. In 2011, a Belgian Malinois (mal-uhn-WAH) named Fitas was on patrol with French soldiers in Afghanistan. As the dog was searching the area, he found fifteen enemy soldiers who were waiting to **ambush** the French troops. The brave dog quickly ran circles around the enemy so that the fighters could not escape. At the same time, the dog alerted the French soldiers so that they could attack.

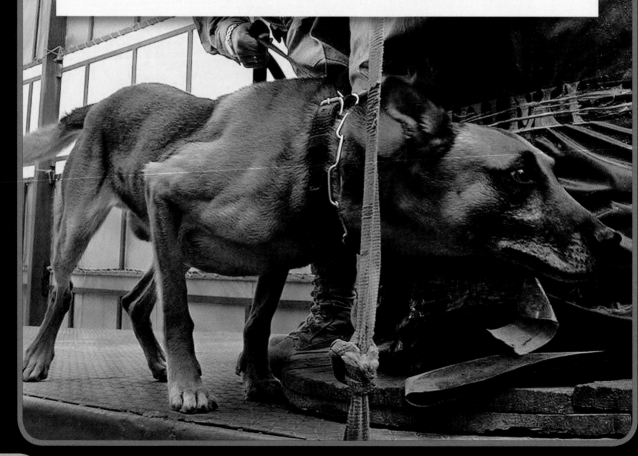

Belgian Malinois, such as the one seen here, are often trained to be military working dogs. They are fast, brave, strong, and smart. They also smell and hear extremely well.

During the battle that followed, Fitas was captured by the enemy. Amazingly, after four months, the heroic dog managed to escape and return to his unit. However, his paw had been badly injured. Sadly, he died the following year from an **infection** that developed as a result of his wound. Fitas's bravery, however, was never forgotten by the troops he helped to save.

The red spot on Fitas's paw shows where he was injured.

In honor of his heroic actions, Fitas was awarded the French Gold Medal of National Defense with the Silver Star.

Taking a Bullet

Military dogs often risk their lives for soldiers. Yet soldiers also take risks to protect their dogs. In 2012, U.S. Army Sergeant Aaron Yoder, a handler, nearly lost his life while trying to save Bart, his black Labrador retriever.

Sergeant Aaron Yoder and his dog, Bart

Sergeant Yoder knew that the enemy often shoots at MWDs because of their sharp bomb-sniffing skills. During a gunfight in Afghanistan with the Taliban, the sergeant used his own body to shield Bart and protect him from danger. While doing so, Yoder himself was shot in the leg. Luckily, he survived. Thanks to Yoder's bravery and loyalty to his dog, Bart was not injured.

Sergeant Yoder was flown to a hospital after being shot in the leg while protecting Bart.

The Taliban is a **militant** Islamic group that took control of Afghanistan from the mid-1990s to 2001.

A Double Loss

A dog and its handler share a special closeness. If the handler is injured or killed in battle, the dog feels pain and loss. A powerful example of this strong bond can be seen in the relationship between Theo, a dog that served in the British army, and his handler, Lance Corporal Liam Tasker.

Lance Corporal Liam Tasker on duty with his dog, Theo

During a five-month period, Tasker and Theo found fourteen hidden bombs and many other dangerous weapons in Afghanistan. Sadly, Tasker was killed in battle in 2011. Shortly after the soldier's body was taken away for burial, Theo had a **seizure** and died. Friends who knew the pair believe that Theo's seizure may have been caused by the deep sadness he felt over the loss of his handler.

Lance Corporal Liam Tasker taking time to relax with Theo

A dog can become **depressed** after losing its owner. The sadness can weaken the dog's appetite and **immune system**, leaving the animal less able to fight an infection that might develop in its body.

Easing the Pain

Not all military dog stories end as sadly as Theo's. Sometimes, a dog can provide comfort to the family of a soldier who has died. That's what happened in the case of Conrad Lewis, a British **paratrooper**. While serving in Afghanistan in 2011, he found a stray dog and named her Peg. Lewis took care of Peg, sharing his food and taking her on patrol. He hoped to keep Peg as a pet upon returning home to England, but a **sniper** shot and killed him.

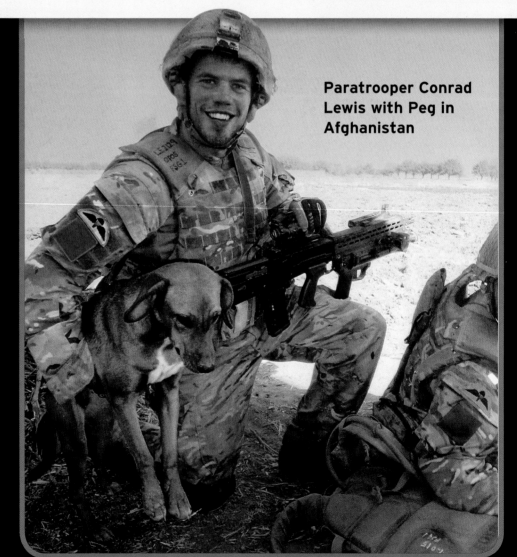

Paratrooper Conrad Lewis with Peg in Afghanistan

Lewis's parents knew how much Peg had meant to their son. They wanted to honor his wishes by adopting his best friend, so they arranged to have Peg brought back to England. After a six-month **quarantine**, Peg began her new life with the Lewises. Conrad's parents, Tony and Sandi Lewis, said that having Peg made them feel as if their son was watching over them.

Conrad's parents, Tony and Sandi Lewis, with Peg

Stray dogs that are brought from one country to another may be required to undergo a quarantine to make sure the animal has no diseases that might spread to people or to other animals.

Together Again

The happiest soldier and dog stories end with the dog and its handler being reunited after both complete their military service. That's what happened to U.S. Marine Corporal Megan Leavey and her bomb-sniffing German shepherd, Sergeant Rex. The two of them had gone on more than 100 missions together in search of explosives in Iraq. In 2006, however, a bomb blast badly injured Corporal Leavey, ending her military career.

Marine Corporal Megan Leavey on patrol with her dog, Sergeant Rex

Meanwhile, Sergeant Rex continued to serve in the Marines. Yet Leavey never lost hope of adopting the dog. Six years later, when Sergeant Rex finally retired, the military granted Leavey her wish. After the dog was checked to make sure it was tame enough to be adopted, Rex was allowed to live with Leavey and her two other dogs in New York.

In the past, all retired MWDs were put to sleep. It was believed that the dogs were too **aggressive** to become household pets. In 2000, however, a law was passed that allows people to adopt the dogs after they retire.

Corporal Leavey and her dog were honored at a baseball game at Yankee Stadium in 2012.

23

Trying to Cope

Most soldiers' dogs offer their help during wartime. Yet some canines help soldiers deal with emotional problems once they've returned home. Just ask Andrew Pastusic. He was a U.S. Army sergeant in Iraq when a bomb hit his truck. The attack was so frightening that Andrew became afraid to drive any kind of vehicle again.

A U.S. soldier stands next to a burning military truck after it was attacked near an airport in Iraq.

Upon returning home to Texas in 2009, Andrew grew depressed. He stayed inside most of the time, watching television and avoiding people. Doctors diagnosed him as having post-traumatic stress disorder, or PTSD. Could a dog help him cope with his problems?

The extreme dangers of war can cause soldiers to develop emotional problems after they return home. A person with PTSD often prefers to remain alone rather than face other people.

Post-traumatic stress disorder is an illness that causes a person to feel very sad, nervous, and afraid. The person may suffer nightmares, loss of memory, and a fear of public places.

A Soldier's Best Friend

To help overcome his fears, Andrew began taking classes in a program based in San Antonio, Texas, called Train a Dog—Save a Warrior. The classes showed Andrew how to train his chocolate Labrador retriever, Cocoa, to become a **service dog**. While Andrew taught Cocoa, the dog immediately helped her owner to relax simply by being a friendly and loving companion. After their first class together, Andrew found the courage to drive with Cocoa in his car for forty-five minutes.

After his first drive with Cocoa, Andrew said, "I looked at Cocoa snuggled close to me on the front seat and she looked up at me and seemed to be telling me that I was going to be okay."

Andrew training Cocoa

Today, Cocoa remains an enormous help and comfort to the former soldier. If Andrew has a nightmare, Cocoa licks his face to wake him. "That dog saved my life," said Andrew. On or off the battlefield, a dog clearly can become a soldier's best friend.

Andrew gets a kiss from Cocoa.

Just the Facts

- In 2011, about 600 military working dogs served in Afghanistan and Iraq. More than 2,000 dogs were stationed on other U.S. military bases around the world.

- Military working dogs at Lackland Air Force Base are trained to serve in the U.S. Army, Navy, Air Force, and Marine Corps.

- Without the help of dogs, U.S. soldiers in Afghanistan and Iraq usually find about 50 percent of the roadside bombs hidden by the enemy. However, when MWDs patrol with the soldiers, the teams find about 80 percent of the bombs.

- Some veterinarians believe that dogs, like humans, can develop post-traumatic stress disorder. A dog with PTSD may become nervous and afraid. Therapy for depressed dogs includes walks with friendly people.

- MWDs become very attached to the people with whom they work. If a dog needs to change its handler, it can take several weeks for the animal to learn to trust someone new.

Geri relaxes with his handler, Senior Airman Stephen Hanks.

Common Breeds: SOLDIERS' DOGS

Labrador retriever

Golden retriever

German shepherd

Belgian Malinois

adopt (uh-DOPT) to take into one's family

aggressive (uh-GRESS-iv) acting in a fierce or threatening way

ambush (AM-bush) to attack from a hidden position

armed forces (ARMD FORSS-iz) the military groups a country uses to protect itself

base (BAYSS) the place where soldiers live or operate from

bond (BOND) to form a close friendship or connection

canine (KAY-nine) a member of the dog family

cells (SELZ) basic, very tiny parts of a person, animal, or plant

compound (KOM-pound) a fenced-in area with buildings inside

consciousness (KON-shuhss-nuhss) being awake and able to think

depressed (di-PREST) very sad

explosives (ek-SPLOH-sivz) things that can blow up, such as bombs

handler (HAND-lur) a person who works with and trains dogs or other animals

immeasurable (i-MEZH-ur-uh-buhl) too great to be measured

immune system (i-MYOON SISS-tuhm) the system that protects one's body against disease and infection

infection (in-FEK-shuhn) an illness caused by germs or viruses

loyal (LOI-uhl) faithful to others

Marine Corps (muh-REEN KOR) a branch of the U.S. military whose members are trained to fight on land, at sea, and in the air

militant (MIL-uh-tuhnt) prepared to fight fiercely for a belief or cause

military (MIL-uh-*ter*-ee) the fighting forces of a country

paratrooper (PA-ruh-*troo*-pur) a soldier who is trained to jump by parachute into battle

patrol (puh-TROHL) walking or traveling around an area to protect it

quarantine (KWOR-uhn-teen) a period in which a person or animal is kept separated from others in order to stop a disease from spreading

scents (SENTS) smells

seizure (SEE-zhur) a sudden attack or illness

service dog (SUR-viss DAWG) a dog that is trained to help a person who is disabled in some way

shrapnel (SHRAP-nuhl) small pieces of metal scattered by an exploding bomb or other device

sniper (SNIPE-ur) a person who fires at enemy fighters from a hidden place

stray dogs (STRAY DAWGZ) dogs without owners

tourniquet (TUR-nuh-kuht) a bandage or piece of cloth twisted tightly around a part of a person's body to stop a wound from bleeding

unit (YOO-nit) a group of soldiers who are part of a larger group

Bibliography

Dowling, Mike. *Sergeant Rex: The Unbreakable Bond Between a Marine and His Military Working Dog.* New York: Atria Books (2011).

Goodavage, Maria. *Soldier Dogs: The Untold Story of America's Canine Heroes.* New York: Dutton (2012).

Rogak, Lisa. *The Dogs of War: The Courage, Love, and Loyalty of Military Working Dogs.* New York: St. Martin's Griffin (2012).

Swan, Madeline. *Dogs at War: Canine Heroes of Outstanding Courage and Bravery.* London: Max Press (2010).

Read More

Apte, Sunita. *Combat-Wounded Dogs (Dog Heroes).* New York: Bearport (2010).

Goldish, Meish. *Bomb-Sniffing Dogs (Dog Heroes).* New York: Bearport (2012).

Goldish, Meish. *War Dogs (America's Animal Soldiers).* New York: Bearport (2012).

Murray, Julie. *Military Animals (Going to Work).* Edina, MN: ABDO (2009).

Ruffin, Frances E. *Military Dogs (Dog Heroes).* New York: Bearport (2007).

Learn More Online

Visit these Web sites to learn more about soldiers' dogs:

http://usmilitary.about.com/od/jointservices/a/militarydogs.htm

www.jbmf.us/cur-wot.aspx

www.jbmf.us/hst-ww1.aspx

www.militaryworkingdogadoptions.com

www.petcentric.com/Videos/Video/Snouts-in-Your-Town-Military-Dogs.aspx?videoid=1217379866001

www.uswardogs.org

Index

About the Author

Meish Goldish has written more than 200 books for children. His book *Heart-Stopping Roller Coasters* was a Children's Choices selection in 2011. He lives in Brooklyn, New York

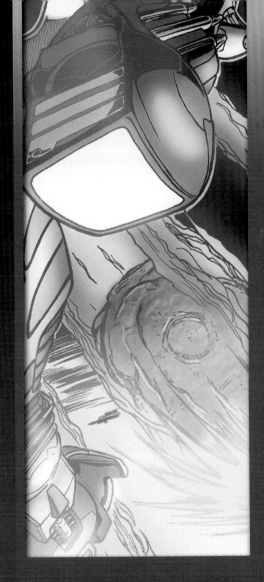

If there's a line, he'll cross it; if there's a knot, he'll cut it; if there's a risk, he'll take it... smiling. In his solitary world, there's no room for second thoughts, no margin for error. "Out there" is a permanent state of mind, and the more impossible, downright insane the mission, the better this daredevil AUTOBOT likes it. His name...

... IS HOT ROD.

THE TRANSFORMERS: SPOTLIGHT: HOT ROD

WRITTEN BY: SIMON FURMAN
ART BY: NICK ROCHE
COLORS BY: LIAM SHALLOO
COVER ART BY: NICK ROCHE & JAMES RAIZ
LETTERS BY: ROBBIE ROBBINS
EDITS BY: DAN TAYLOR

Licensed by: Hasbro Properties Group

Special thanks to Hasbro's Aaron Archer, Elizabeth Griffin, and Richard Zambarano for their invaluable assistance.

Spotlight

VISIT US AT
www.abdopublishing.com

Reinforced library bound edition published in 2008 by Spotlight, a division of the ABDO Publishing Group, 8000 West 78th Street, Edina, Minnesota 55439. Published by agreement with IDW Publishing. www.idwpublishing.com

Library of Congress Cataloging-in-Publication Data

Furman, Simon.
  Hot Rod / written by Simon Furman ; art by Nick Roche ; colors by Liam Shalloo ; cover art by Nick Roche & James Raiz ; letters by Robbie Robbins.
     p. cm. -- (The transformers: spotlight)
  ISBN 978-1-59961-474-8
  1. Graphic novels. I. Roche, Nick. II. Shalloo, Liam. III. Title.

PN6727.F87H68 2008
741.5'973--dc22

2007033982

All Spotlight books have reinforced library bindings and are manufactured in the United States of America.

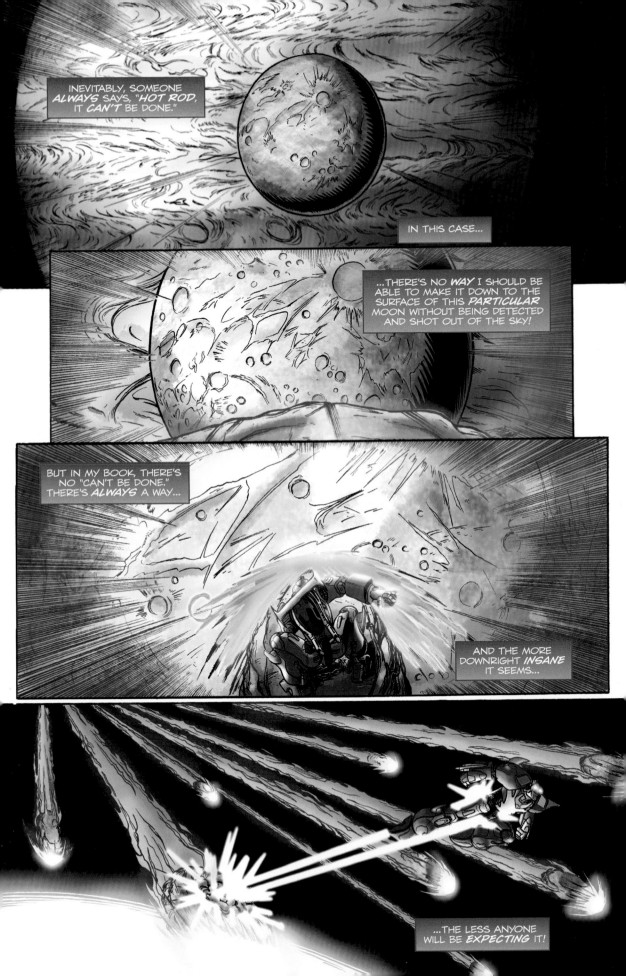

LEAVING MY "RIDE" TO IMPACT ON THE SURFACE, I *FREEFALL*, ALL BUT THE MOST ESSENTIAL SYSTEMS OFFLINE, JUST ANOTHER BIT OF SPACE DEBRIS.

I'M OUT ON MY OWN, UP AGAINST *IMPOSSIBLE* ODDS, MY LIFE—AND MY LIFE ALONE—ON THE LINE.

IT'S A *RUSH!*

NO WAY TO KNOW WHERE THE SENSOR BUFFER BEGINS AND ENDS, SO I LEAVE IT TO THE LAST *POSSIBLE* MOMENT...

...TO POWER UP AND GENERATE THE *NULL FIELD*.

EVEN SO...

...IT'S A *FAR* FROM GENTLE LANDING.

THUST

I FLIRT WITH *CRITICAL* SYSTEM-SHOCK, DIPPING IN AND OUT OF CONSCIOUSNESS.

I TRY TO *FOCUS*... ON THE *MISSION*, ON THE *OBJECTIVE*, BUT INSTEAD...

I *SLIP*...

...OF THE *OMEGA BUNKER*.

RIGHT. BORE DRONES ONE AND TWO ARE IN POSITION. LET'S GO TO WORK...

GIZMO?

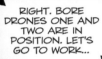

I'LL HAVE THE *HOLOMATTER PROJECTOR* UP AND RUNNING IN JUST A FEW NANO-KLIKS. STAND BY...

BACKBEAT?

SETTING LOW-YIELD *CHARGES*. TIMERS ARE SYNCHED WITH GIZMO'S HOLOPROGRAM.

DEALER?

DROPSHIP UPLINK ALIGNED AND LOCKED.

HAVE BORE DRONE THREE LOCK ONTO MY POSITION AND BACKTRACK.

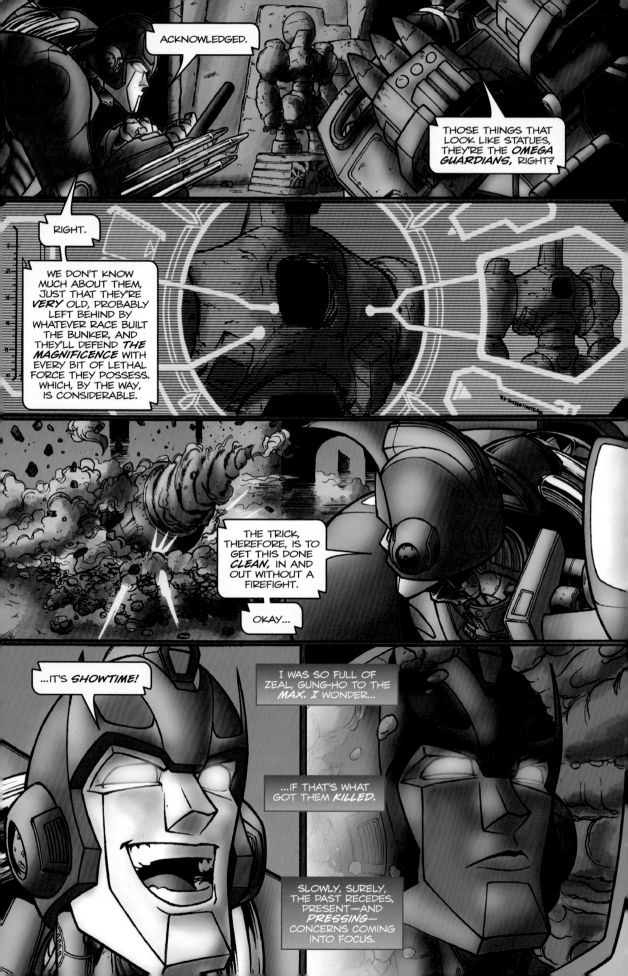

...I MAKE MY *MOVE!*

THE INVASIVE PROGRAM PROPAGATES AN APPARENTLY RANDOM, BUT IN REALITY RIGOROUSLY *TIMED* SEQUENCE OF "GHOST" ALERTS AND SENSOR BLACK SPOTS.

AND, AS GUARDS AND TROUBLESHOOTERS ARE PULLED THIS WAY AND THAT, I...

...SLIP THROUGH THE *GAPS.*

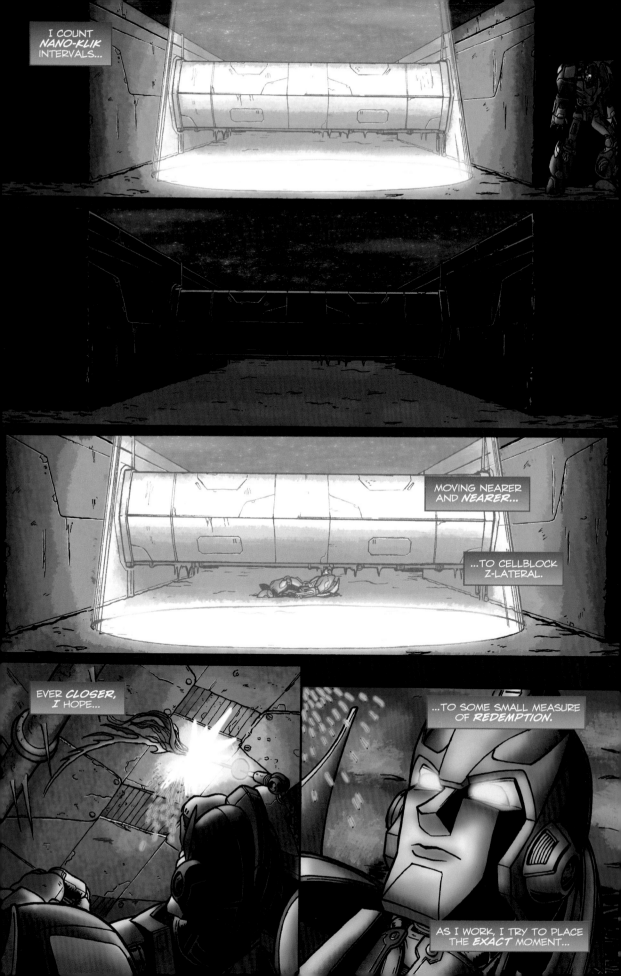

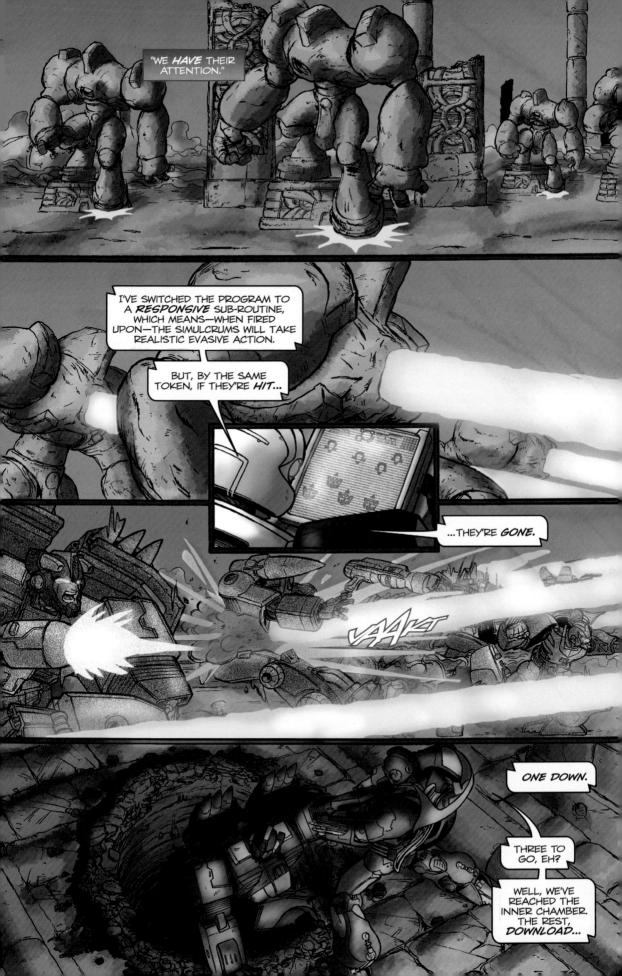

"WE *HAVE* THEIR ATTENTION."

I'VE SWITCHED THE PROGRAM TO A *RESPONSIVE* SUB-ROUTINE, WHICH MEANS—WHEN FIRED UPON—THE SIMULCRUMS WILL TAKE REALISTIC EVASIVE ACTION.

BUT, BY THE SAME TOKEN, IF THEY'RE *HIT*...

...THEY'RE *GONE*.

ONE DOWN.

THREE TO GO, EH?

WELL, WE'VE REACHED THE INNER CHAMBER. THE REST, *DOWNLOAD*...

...ARE MERCIFULLY DROWNED OUT BY A CACOPHONY OF STYX ALARM KLAXONS, AS—ON *CUE*...

...THE VIRUS POPS *EVERY* CELL DOOR IN THE CONTAINMENT BLOCKS.

KIND OF ITS *LAST HURRAH.*

STANDARD PROCEDURE, IN SUCH AN EVENTUALITY...

THIS IS A *CODE-NINE.* I REPEAT...

...IS TO EVACUATE *ALL* HIGH RANKING OFFICERS TO A SECURE ORBITAL RELAY PLATFORM.

I GUESS THEY FIGURE EVEN IF THE PRISONERS GET OUT, THERE'S *NOWHERE* FOR THEM TO GO.

SO *THE BRASS* JUST GETS OUT OF HARM'S WAY AND WAITS FOR A CLEAN-UP SQUAD.

IT'S MY *TICKET* OUT OF HERE!

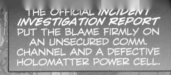

THE OFFICIAL *INCIDENT INVESTIGATION REPORT* PUT THE BLAME FIRMLY ON AN UNSECURED COMM. CHANNEL AND A DEFECTIVE HOLOMATTER POWER CELL.

BUT IT WAS MY RESPONSIBILITY TO DOUBLE-CHECK THE MISSION ORDNANCE AND SECURITY INTERLOCKS.

THOUGH NOBODY EVER ACTUALLY POINTED THE FINGER...

WAIT HERE...

...THE BUCK STOPPED WITH *ME*.

WHAT THE FR–

SURPRISE!

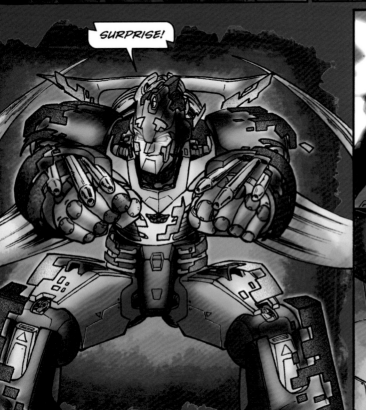

KA-BLAMM